Casino Survival Guide
Breaking the bank!

STEVEN SCHOOL

Casino Survival Guide.

ISBN:1482692678
ISBN-13:9781482692679

DEDICATION

I dedicate this book to fun loving people worldwide.

Casino Survival Guide.

Casino Survival Guide.

CONTENTS

Casino Survival Guide.

ACKNOWLEDGMENTS

I would like to acknowledge casinos worldwide for giving us the place to practice our skills, at your expense of course. Thank you, for the free rooms, meals, and of course, money.

Casino Survival Guide.

1 GETTING STARTED.

Let us plan our trip in advance, calling ahead for room reservations can sometimes result in a discount. Visit your chosen casino website online, see if you can sign up electronically to receive mailers, the casino loves to send you coupons for discounts and freebies and we will begin by taking full advantage of this.

Once inside the casino, the very first thing that we want to do is to sign up at the players club, also ask for an extra club card as well, this will enable us to earn free or discounted rooms, meals, and prizes.

Whenever you wish to play an electronic game, always make sure you have inserted your players club card into the machine first, otherwise you will not be racking up your freebies.

Pick a popular slot machine, preferably a dollar slot with a progressive jackpot, insert your extra club card into this machine and leave it there, other people may come along and play, inadvertently racking up freebies for you on your players club account, always remember to retrieve your card later.

If you are going to play a table game, simply hand your club card to the dealer so that he or she can record your point accrual for you.

Once you have actually set up your players club account and played in the casino, they will start mailing you great coupons for your next visit.

Many casinos will have cocktail waitresses wandering around serving free drinks, I have a couple of tips about this, these places are hoping that the cheap booze will be just enough to cloud your thinking and get you onto a nice long losing streak, so I highly recommend avoiding the alcoholic beverages, the waitress will soon begin to ignore you if you do not regularly tip her. We are here to win, just as an athlete competing to win a triathlon.

So I recommend just ordering water or juice, lets us stay well hydrated and keep our brain cells operating at peak performance.

If you get tired, you will not be thinking clearly, this is a great time to retire to your room for a good night of sleep, and get well rested so that we can return fresh tomorrow, and show the dealers who is boss, that's right, who is your daddy?, I am, that's who! And I fully intend to win, and win big.

In it, to win it, that is the name of the game, that is what we are here for, to start small, and rake in huge piles of chips, while getting compensated for free rooms, and free meals, that is right, pay me to break the bank, and clean house.

If you plan your casino vacation trip during major holidays the room rates usually are at peak prices, if you avoid these times, possibly calling in your reservations in advance of course, and choosing the off season times, you are much more likely to get free or heavily discounted lodging.

I save my change year round, and use that as my gaming funds, simply just bring it all in, unrolled and unwrapped to the casino and any of the cashier stations will quickly count it and exchange it for cash or gaming tokens, they have machines that they simply dump all of the bulk coinage into, these machines will effectively sort and count your coins very quickly, and total up the amount you are owed, these machines are very fast, efficient, and reliable. I feel that this is a good method of budgeting what I am willing to gamble with, I never will dispense with my credit card, or withdraw bank funds to gamble with, I set limits for myself in this area, after all, I am here to generate cold hard cash, not bankrupt myself and drain my accounts. I feel that one hundred dollars is plenty enough money for gaming, no matter how long I intend to stay and gamble, one hundred dollars is plenty enough for me to get the ball rolling and get into the profit margin, if I cannot successfully work within this budget, then there is no need to lose any more money than this. Once I get up to the three hundred dollar mark, I now keep two hundred dollars in my hand for gaming, all winnings above this go into my pocket, and will be going home with me. This is part of my strategy, at the three hundred dollar mark, I pocket my original one hundred dollars, and I now have two hundred dollars of the casino money to gamble with, from here on out, I play with their money, and not my own.

I will see just how big of an amount of cash I can build this into, some people will keep dipping into their own funds, to continue playing during a losing streak, possibly spending thousands of dollars that in this day and age, we simply cannot afford to lose, I would much rather withdraw my funds from the casino bank, in the form of winning the games.

Bus trips, sometimes you can find package deals wherein overland transportation is provided to and from the casino from major cities, usually these are very low cost, and they generally come with coupons and vouchers for free gaming tokens, discounted or free meals, and discounted rooms, you might also receive access to shows at free or discounted prices. These bus trip packages can be very lucrative as generally speaking, the cost of round trip fuel would probably cost you more than this entire package, not to mention the bonuses. There are many casino's available these days, and they vary a little, in my experience some of the ones at Indian reservations usually are not too hard to find, I have done well at these, I have also been to Biloxi, Reno, Las Vegas, Sparks, and Virginia city.

Some of the old time saloons in Virginia city had several vintage antique slot machines, I really like finding these. Several years ago I read an old article somewhere which stated that if you find an old three wheel slot machine with the cherry symbol sitting directly on the pay line in the center column, that it is supposedly a sign that this machine is ready to pay out a jackpot, I have thus always kept an eye out for this and I have always done well with it, so in my opinion this is a valid tip, however these machines are becoming rather difficult to find in our era of modern machines. I have in fact won several payouts over the years using this bit of information. I have seen many tips on betting strategies, one of them is to double or triple your bet every time that you lose, then when you win you revert to betting the minimum bet, I do not usually recommend this technique as a main staple because it can lead to huge losses, it does however has its place once in a while which I will cover in the roulette section. In my opinion, winning and losing usually runs in streaks, I believe that when a winning streak appears, bet big. I roll with it until I suffer one loss and then I revert back to the minimum bet, if after a few hands the winning streak does not return, then I simply move on to another game. I will switch from blackjack to roulette to slots, and vice versa. I will usually however begin with the slot machines.

GOALS.

It is important to first consider and outline your goals before even setting foot on this type of excursion. How much money can you afford to spend?, how much are you willing to lose?, how much do you expect to win?, I mean realistically speaking, what is an amount of money, that you would be happy enough with winning, to simply quit gambling cold turkey, and walk away from the table? Many people get really excited when they win a few hundred dollars or more, the issue is that they do not know when to stop. If you keep playing, eventually you will hit a losing streak and end up giving your winnings right back to the house. When this happens, some persons will mistakenly believe that if they just use the Atm machine, withdraw some additional cash and continue playing, that they will win it all back and more.

This is usually not the case, you have to know when to quit, no strategy is foolproof, there is no secret strategy which works every time, all we can do is increase our chances of winning with smart betting, coupled with knowing when to walk away. I myself learned this from experience, I have started with one hundred dollars, built it up to a few thousand, and then paid it all right back because I did not yet know when to walk away. This is why I set goals for myself. There have been many times that I won several hundred dollars at one game, but I now have more streamlined rules. I would rather win three or four hundred dollars at one game, and walk away, than to win perhaps nine hundred dollars, continue playing, and give it all right back to the house. So with table games If I begin with one hundred dollars, once I am anywhere between the three to four hundred dollar mark, I will quit that game and walk away cold turkey, no matter what. I will then either switch to a different game, or simply just take a break. I have decided that if I can show a two hundred dollar profit from one game, that I am perfectly happy with this number, this is a good profit and there are still many other games to play, I can always return to this game later for a few more hands, starting over of course, refusing to dip into my winnings which are definitely going to go home with me. I start with one hundred dollars and that is it, if that hundred bucks dwindles down to twenty or thirty dollars I am done gambling, finished. I will not even lose my entire hundred dollars, you should be cheap here, we are in it for a win, not a loss. However at my current level of experience it will be a rare day indeed if I do not come out ahead. The casinos take quick notice of me when I begin to play, not because they know me, it is simply because I win their money and they do not like that. I know the meaning of the word integrity, it is one of my favorite words, and I follow all the rules of the game.

KNOW YOUR GAME.

The most important thing, is to know your game. You must know all the rules, and you must be at expert level before you begin playing with real money. The casino would just love for a beginner to step up to the table and begin learning the hard way while the house rakes in all of your cash, believe me, that dealer is put through a training program, he or she is going to be playing at expert level before the casino ever even lets them begin working a live table game. They are also fully trained in every possible known strategy that has ever been applied to that game. You may hear them call out key words to their supervisor such as progression, this lets the higher up know that you are here to win, and that you have invested some time and thought into how you are going to play. Since the dealer is an expert in this particular game, so must you also be. I train at home using realistic casino type video games, I use these extensively to thoroughly test my strategies and theories, and to ingrain my techniques into my memory until it has become as a natural reflex. If I plan to head to the casino, you can surely believe that I will have fully warmed up and honed my skills at home first. I will fully refresh and revitalize my techniques on the home video game system, keeping myself up to date. My methods of smart betting are very simple, yet I will insure that I am playing at peak performance, before even heading out of the house. I also have a smart phone with internet capabilities and I have downloaded several free casino games which I can play anywhere, anytime, I even have two different roulette games in my phone, I also have a real roulette wheel at home.

It has taken me thirty years of gaming to develop my techniques, and i believe that if everyone followed my advice the casinos would end up going out of business. Those businesses do not want you to have the information that I present, I can easily win five thousand in about two to three hours.

I have two modes of play, passive and aggressive. Normally I integrate myself into the flow of casino play with the passive method, which is to say that I will walk through the casino starting from the players club desk with my new club cards, I will examine the type of games that are present and where they are, as I walk I will sample the best looking slot machines, to me these are twenty five cent, and one dollar progressive jackpot slots. I will pick my machines and play three rounds each at maximum bet, if I hit a jackpot I will pocket it, and continue my walk, working my way over to the table games, I also love video blackjack, progression techniques seem to work very well with these, that is probably why these machines seem to be getting harder to find.

Once at the tables I will choose either blackjack or roulette, in either order, and I will be playing both games, betting low since I am in passive mode, this means that I am betting anywhere from five to fifteen dollars per individual bet, I will play three rounds to determine if I am in a winning, or losing streak. If it is a losing streak I will switch to a different game, however if it is a winning streak I will continue to play and I will switch to aggressive mode. This means that I am going to begin betting high amounts because I am winning, a winning streak does not last forever in one game, I could probably stay longer and win more, but I want to walk away before I hit that losing streak, keeping my profit in my pocket, building it up, so that I have something to invest for my future, get that money working for me and building interest. When my per game profit is anywhere from two to three hundred dollars, I will usually walk away, however I have been known to stay longer once in a while, even to the five thousand mark at one roulette game.

Many so called professional gamblers will tell you that you need a huge bankroll in order to sustain you through the losing streaks, that is simply not true and is very poor business advice, that is one key point where my advice is different, and better. As I told you before winning and losing runs in streaks, the goal of business is to make money, not to spend it!

Therefore one key method of my casino play is that I will avoid the losing streaks, this is a financial fight between us and the casino, and my wallet does not need to take a beating. So bring you're A game to the table!, I avoid the long losing streaks simply because I play three hands, at this point I already know if I am in the winning streak, or the losing streak. If I am winning, I will place a large bet, such as the maximum table wager allowed, each time I win I will place a new bet, half the size of the previous bet, this way each time I win, I am pulling back some of the casinos money into my pocket. If I am in the losing streak I simply move to a different game. There is no need to stay here and attempt to endure the financial beating of a losing streak, simply moving to a new table changes this completely, in fact, if you are losing at one table, you could do no worse than that at a different table, but you have a fifty fifty chance of changing from a losing streak, to a winning streak by doing so. All you have to do is learn to quickly recognize whether each game is in the winning or losing streak, and adjust accordingly. I will in fact very quickly identify a game that is in the winning mode, from my three gaming groups of blackjack, slot machines, and roulette. These are the games that I practice, and practice makes perfect, therefore with this grouping of three, I have plenty of options at a casino.

BLACKJACK.

The goal of blackjack is to achieve the total score of twenty one points in your first hand of two cards, this is a natural blackjack. If we are dealt a lesser number we can ask for an additional card or more to increase our number, however we may risk busting which is an automatic loss if our total score is above twenty one points. This is something that we need to avoid and leave to the dealer. As we discussed before, winning and losing runs in streaks, and so also in the particular game of blackjack, busting also tends to run in streaks. Since we already know that winning and losing runs in streaks, and we now have learned how to recognize these streaks, all we really want to do is to bet small at first to determine which streak we are in, then avoid the losing streaks, bet high in the winning streaks, and know when to walk away with a profit in hand, before the streak changes and reverts back to a losing streak, never ever, try to ride out a losing streak, just simply walk away from it, cut it loose, and go find another winning streak somewhere else. So in this game of blackjack we first want to find the table that is in the winning streak, then we want to bet high and play the basic strategy of this particular game, while at the same time refusing to bust, always leave that to the dealer. If I have an eleven, I will hit, if I have a twelve I will stand, this may be hard to digest at first but realize that I will never bust, and the dealer loves to bust in streaks. I will not split a pair of tens because this is already a winning hand and it could easily be turned into two losing hands by splitting. I will always split pairs of aces and eights, these are usually losing hands, that can easily be split into two winning hands. I also never buy insurance in blackjack. The biggest hope that the dealer has is that you do not know how to play the game very well, and his or her personal goal, something that their trainers and bosses have ingrained into their mind until it becomes instinct, like a natural reflex, is to do everything they can to make you bust, do not give them the satisfaction. After all, this is war, it is about money, and therefore it is personal. Bring your Kevlar wallet and prepare to fight! We do not need to tip the dealer, it does not increase your chances of winning, also pay close attention to the stacks of winning chips that they use to pay you with, I have actually seen a dealer try to slip one dollar chips into my winning payout of ten dollars chips.

Always ignore idle talk if the dealer tries to engage you in conversation, they are trying to break your concentration, and to change your method of play in order to get you into a nice long losing streak, this is what they are trained to do, simply ignore it. Have you ever heard the saying anything you say can and will be used against you in a court of law?, well it applies here in the casino in a similar form, any form of conversation between you and the dealer will be used to cause you to lose, so completely ignore them. The reason that I stopped tipping them is threefold, number one, it does not affect my chance of winning, number two, it causes me to lose because I am literally giving my money away to them, and three because their job is to cause me to lose my money, therefore if they did not win it from me, it is squarely mine and needs to stay in my pocket. You do not need to tip every single person that you interact with, there are situations however where I will tip, and when I do I am very generous. I tend to be very giving in all aspects of my life. If I see a person who does not have money to buy a meal or pay a bill I will gladly pay it for them if it is within my means and I have done it many times even up to the amount of five hundred dollars, paying a bill for an acquaintance. I believe that it is good karma, that it is good to be helpful and generous in this world. That does not mean bringing homeless people into your home, but it does not hurt to give them food, clothing, beverages, cash, whatever they need. One day on my way to work I stopped to buy a breakfast burrito, as I began to eat it in my car I noticed a homeless man staring at me, I gave him twenty dollars and he was very happy with this, twenty bucks is nothing, but it was something to him. Now back to the blackjack, I will approach the table, I always prefer to find one that already has two or three players, I will bet anywhere from five to fifteen dollars to get the ball rolling, I will play three hands. This is enough for me to determine if I am in the winning streak, if I am, I will bet the maximum bet. If it wins then I will now bet half of the maximum bet, thus putting casino money back into my pocket with every win. I will continue this until I revert back to ten or fifteen dollar bets, as long as I am winning I will keep playing these small bets until the losing hand strikes one time, I will then move on to another game. I will keep my little jackpot in my pocket and find the next winning streak at a new game, frequently switching from slot machines to roulette, to blackjack. Many people believe in a strategy called progression, I have used it extensively and determined that most of the time it is unwise and result in huge losses, progression does however have its usefulness in certain situations which we will discuss. It is simply to double or triple your bet every time you lose, in the hopes that a win will shortly come along, paying you back all of your money, plus a small profit. This technique quickly exceeds the maximum table bet and therefore usually results in huge irrecoverable losses, the casino puts a limit on the betting amount for the specific purpose of defeating the progression strategy. You can however simply reverse it, which I have already explained by betting big in the winning streak, with each win you simply reduce your bet by half, this can be a very effective winning tool. Sometimes however progression does suit me well, and I will explain that in the roulette section.

SLOT MACHINES.

Slot machines can be a lot of fun, I have played many of them over the years and have my favorites, I also have learned a thing or two which can help you. Several years ago in Reno Nevada, I was touring the casinos, sampling the games as I like to do, I found three very interesting slot machines which I played. I learned something very specific about these particular three games that I will share with you now. All three were at different casinos, I played them all in the same evening, the first was a bank of video gaming machines, video poker to be exact, which I am not very good at anyway. The thing however that drew me to this usually undesirable game was the fact that on top of this rectangular shaped bank of games, was sitting a red ferrari, I love this automobile and the sign said that a player could in fact, actually win the car, I however won nothing here, at the next casino was a similar set up, but this one had a fully restored 1965 convertible mustang on top, I also won nothing here. Now the third casino had an old style slot machine where you pull the handle and the reels spin, on top of this machine, instead of having the usual painted or colored glass, it had a window. Inside this window was an old black miniature toy train setup on tracks, it had a mining theme set among tiny mountains. The open cars of this train were filled with one ounce silver bars and small gold coins. This attracted me like a powerful magnet, I was drawn to this machine, envisioning myself winning gold and silver, I however won absolutely nothing here. Slot machines can be loose, or tight. Which means that they can pay out often, or rarely. These three machines that I have just described to you, are designed to subliminally attract you to them, and to make you think that you are going to win big, however these are the tightest machines around, and while they sure look appealing, they are most likely only going to result in losses so I say if you must try your three hands fine, but then move on, I myself prefer to skip them entirely. These are generally referred to as a tourist trap type of game, for weekend warriors, not for the seasoned veteran who knows better.

When you first walk in to a casino, usually you will immediately be faced with a square shaped bank of slot machines blocking your path, there are usually either two or three machines on each of the four sides. This is strategically placed here for a very good reason, you see these machines, at a large fancy casino, are usually rather loose, which means the casino wants you to hit a few jackpots here for two reasons, number one, a win here will get you excited and draw you further into the casino, farther into the spiders web so to speak, where they hope you will get the fever and throw all your money away and leave broke, still reeling from the free glasses of cheap booze, the second reason is that people out in the street will see the jingling bells and flashing lights of your small jackpot and it will attract them into the spiders web as well. What I do with these machines is that after I have enrolled in the players club, I will play my three hands at each of them, keep whatever jackpots I have accrued, and walk away. I also will not put a twenty dollar bill in these machines, the game only wants to gobble it up. Face it, we are in the world of technology now and these machines are actually smart, if I want to bet three dollars, then I will put in that exact amount, pull the handle, and repeat as necessary for my rule of three plays, I believe that by inserting a smaller figure, that this will entice the machine to try and lure me in, that it will try to instill the gambling fever within me, by giving me a small jackpot. I can usually win at least enough here to pay for a nice dinner, and I am not cheap, my favorite restaurant is red lobster and I will ring up a good bill, I even like to bring steak dinners to my rottweilers from fancy steak houses. This is fine fodder for my canines, if the casino wants to be so kind as to cover the bill, then so be it. My animals are picky, they love a good steak and baked potato, but they aren't into seafood. Land sharks aren't used to things that swim, just like sharks don't like the taste of humans, yeah right. Now that we are inside the casino, and the dealers can smell our blood in the water like fresh fish, I will begin my walk, scoping the layout, looking for the types of games that I enjoy, and where they are located. I believe the slots directly facing the table games, also the ones that are lining the pathways through the casino tend to be loose, the reason is that the casino will allow some payouts to keep people interested, some of them being large, but the thing is they want these wins to be visible, they want as many people as possible to see your big win because it gives everyone gambling fever, so that they all will begin throwing their money away. I will find these payouts, because I know where they are generally located, because I will only play each machine three times, and because I bet the maximum amount, I get the larger payout. I use this technique while traversing the pathways which lead to and from the table games, and the other parts of the casino. Bingo, we have a winner, and it is me!, oh look, it is me again! I usually prefer twenty five cent and dollar slots, I like wheel of fortune and progressive jackpots. While I was at a casino in Biloxi Mississippi some years back, I noticed they had a lot of penny machines, I skipped over most of them, then I found one which had a large menu of different games that you could choose from, as I scrolled through the games, examining each one, I noticed that one seemed easier to win at than the others, therefore I chose this game, I inserted one dollar into this machine, after playing for roughly twenty minutes, I had rung it up to ninety dollars, when I pushed the payout button, the game printed out a piece of paper, which I took to the cashier for payment. At this very same casino I also found an interesting bank of slot machines which were strategically placed in a highly visible portion of the casino, these were five cent machines, with progressive jackpots, and they had large fake firecrackers on top. I absolutely love these machines, I continually won several jackpots at these, over the course of a couple of hours, most of the payouts ranged from forty to eighty dollars apiece. I was so excited I flagged my father down and invited him to play.

As a I mentioned before, the antique slot machines with the spinning reels, if it is a three wheel machine, and the cherries symbol is sitting on the pay line of the center wheel, I have heard, and do believe, that this machine is probably ready to pay out a jackpot, it has been this way for me many times, I once found just such a machine in Reno Nevada, it was a nickel machine, I pulled the handle one time and I won eighty dollars for just the initial price of a few nickels.

Old habits die hard and so if I see the modern video version of this machine I will play it as well.

Video blackjack, I love finding these machines, they seem to be getting harder to find and for good reason, they pay out! Progression and reverse progression both seem to work very well with these types of casino gaming machines. I will settle in here for the long haul with a good twenty five cent game, I also do not drink alcohol during or before play, and if I get mentally tired, I will retire to my room for a rest break. If you are going to be gambling for money, it is very important that you are alert, and thinking clearly at all times, making good decisions. When I get tired I start losing, this is a great time to walk away.

I play all versions of blackjack, roulette, and slots, I stick to these three and avoid other games. With slots I prefer wheel of fortune and all types of progressive jackpot machines. I will examine the game first, since I believe that some have better odds of winning than others, and I will also choose my machine by location as well, if it is in a place where it has optimal visibility to the general public, I believe there is a much higher chance of winning here simply because the casino wants to publicize the idea that people are winning here, and that is why when you win a small ten dollar jackpot the machine lights up, with loud sirens and buzzers to create the subliminal idea to others that you have just struck it rich, you are on easy street for life thanks to the casino, and that people who play here, win here.

ROULETTE.

Roulette is definitely my favorite game, when I was younger blackjack was my main staple but all that drastically changed when I took the time to actually learn how to play roulette, and went even further to study the types of bets which can be placed with this game, the payout schedule of each, and the odds of winning versus losing. This game truly is very simple to play, I use what I call smart betting, coupled with progression and reverse progression. I will choose a roulette table that already has one or more customers playing, I will watch a couple of spins in order to get a feel of how the game is playing out.

I will buy in at one hundred dollars worth of five dollar chips, and I will be sure to examine the minimum and maximum bet threshold allowed.

I am noticing also, where is the ball landing on the table?, is it up in the high numbers or down in the low figures?, this information is very important to me, because it will tell me which groupings of bets that I want to start placing. Some wagers in this game have a high probability of losing, and some have a high chance of winning, while no bet is foolproof, I tend to show many repeated wins in this game with my technique of smart betting.

I usually begin this game by placing two fifteen dollar wagers, I always bet this game in groups of two, no other bets are ever placed by me, I will not place one bet, or three bets, but always two. Now if I was to bet on red or black, my chances of winning would be slightly less than fifty percent, the same with betting on whether the ball will land on odd or even, this is because of the zero and double zero, therefore I will not place these types of wagers, if I were to bet on one single number, I would therefore have a huge chance of losing, so I will not place these bets either, however there is a betting technique which I believe will give me a greater than fifty percent chance of winning, in my own personal opinion, my bet may even give me closer to a sixty percent chance or more of winning.

In the game of roulette there are what is known as inside bets, and outside bets, zero and double zero, red or black, there are other betting options as well, but I personally believe that we do not need to be concerned with these, as I only place outside bets, in groups of two, each one of these two bets by itself will cover a dozen numbers, and by placing two of them, I am covering twenty four numbers each game, which is more than half of the numbers on the board.

Therefore my chances of winning are greater than fifty percent with this method, I have done very well with it, many roulette dealers have commented on this during my play, telling me that my technique is very smart and that is exactly why I refer to it as smart betting.

Notice on the roulette board, that directly in front of you there are three outside bets which each cover one dozen numbers, the first of these which is located on your immediate left covers the numbers one through twelve, the second one of these outside bets which is located directly in front of you covers the numbers thirteen through twenty four, and the third grouping which is located directly to your immediate right, covers the numbers twenty five to thirty six.

I will choose two of these, according to where the ball has landed during the previous two plays that occurred before I entered the game. I usually cover thirteen through twenty four, and twenty five through thirty six, this is just my personal preference and I have in fact done very well with it.

I will begin by placing a fifteen dollar bet upon each of these two groups. If I want to play conservatively, I will continue betting this way, however if I decide to switch to an aggressive system of play I will then move on to reverse progression, followed by progression.

Since there are three groups here, and I have chosen to place a fifteen dollar bets upon two of these while ignoring the third, I have in fact wagered a total of thirty dollars, I have a greater than fifty percent chance of winning here, if the ball lands upon any number from thirteen to thirty six, I will be paid forty five dollars, this means that since I initially bet thirty dollars, and I now have forty five dollars, I have shown a profit of fifteen dollars. In my opinion this is not bad at all for something that took about two minutes of my time, and I can play this way for a few hours if I choose to, or I can simply switch to my aggressive method.

In my aggressive technique, during a winning streak I will begin using reverse progression, this means that I will increase my two bets to the maximum table amount allowed, each time I win I will decrease each bet by half, and play again until I get back to my fifteen dollar mark. I will now play a few hands with my bets placed at ten to fifteen dollars apiece, while I wait for the losing streak to hit. When it does come, I will begin using progression, which means that I will increase my bet with each loss so that when I hit a win I will recover my losses plus a small profit.

I can repeat or adjust my technique as necessary. If for some reason the table seems unusually cold, simply walk away and choose a different game.

Also I recommend that when you are playing any table game, if the dealer is switched, walk away and find a new game, when you are winning, the casino definitely takes very quick notice of this, and they will switch the dealer in order to attempt to disrupt your winning streak by breaking your pattern of luck, I myself choose not to play along with this. You also may notice the dealer calling out key words to the pit boss during your winning streak, which may include phrases such as progression or reverse progression. this marks the point in time that the casino has taken notice of the fact that you came here to win, and that you have invested some thought and training into your methods and techniques of exactly how you are going to do so, it signifies that they are acknowledging the fact that they are playing against an expert, and that there is a high probability that you are going to accrue financial gains here, which means losses for them. They will now scrutinize you more closely to make sure that you are following all the rules. They know full well that it has now become a battle over who will take home the prize. When they switch the dealer, I walk. I also set my loss and win goals before entering or leaving the game, I only invest one hundred dollars throughout the entire range of play covering all three of my types of games that I play. If my one hundred dollars is lost, I am finished playing and this is my loss limit of how much money I am willing to risk. I will also choose a specific amount at each game that I would be happy with winning, and when I hit this goal I walk away keeping my profit in my pocket.

Generally speaking, if my profit per gaming session has reached anywhere from two hundred, to three hundred and fifty dollars, I will choose a specific point somewhere in here to quit and leave this game.

I will now pocket my original investment, as well as a good portion of my winnings, and so I will now be gambling with casino money.

Keep following the winning streaks, and keep walking away from the losing streaks. I myself do not place large wagers until I have won the funds to do so from the casino, I could easily have a few thousand dollars in my hand to play with, but you can safely bet that only one hundred dollars of it came out of my pocket, and that the rest of it is current winnings.

INVEST YOUR WINNINGS.

I believe in investing money for the future, I think that money could be out there working for me and creating more money. The goal of business is to make money, in fact we want to make as much profit as possible, while minimizing our expenditures. My personal goal of business is not to work or to spend money, but just to make money, so once you are hitting the winning streaks let us think about some options of what we can do with that money.

I myself like to invest conservatively, I like an interest bearing savings account, I like to have more than one of them, at different banks.

I also learned from my wise grandfather, about discover bank online. One can open an interest bearing money market account here, and transfer money to and from this account, all from the home computer. I personally liked the fact that I was earning interest, while my principal was not locked down, and I could withdraw my funds at any time, simply by transferring the money electronically, right back into my personal checking account.

You can also write a book about your casino experiences, I started out by simply typing publish books, into the search engine on my home computer. I quickly found a great resource online which was of great help in getting started. I now have published several books which are available in many parts of the world, and I will be publishing more books as well, in fact, I have set a personal goal for myself, that I would like to publish one hundred books. Of course once I achieve this goal, I will undoubtedly set a higher mark.

I have also used some of my funds to embark upon other endeavors, I have opened a lucrative drain cleaning business, and I am a Rottweiler breeder. These animals are very protective, and they multiply hundred dollar bills.
Drain cleaning itself tends to be a high paying industry, most professional drain cleaning technicians nationwide can normally average one thousand dollars per day in sales, with most of it being profit since this type of work is mostly labor, and usually requiring few materials or parts.

OTHER BOOKS BY STEVEN SCHOOL.

Here is a list of other books I have written.

Karate Secrets Revealed.
Grandmas Delicious Recipes.
Trophy Wife.
How To Make Money.
Alchemy And The Green Lion.
Alchemy And The Golden Water.
Alchemy And The Peacocks Tail.
Alchemy Survival Guide.

CASINO SURVIVAL GUIDE.

www.ingramcontent.com/pod-product-compliance
Lightning Source LLC
Chambersburg PA
CBHW051423170526
45165CB00004BA/1936